P9-CCL-682

SOUTH SHORE SCHOOL
MEDIA CENTER

SOUTH SHORE ELEMENTARY SCHOOL

32122133690   92 ALEXANDER
Meet Shaun Alexander :

SOUTH SHORE SCHOOL
MEDIA CENTER

All-Star Players™

MEET SHAUN ALEXANDER

Football's Top Running Back

John Smithwick

PowerKiDS press

New York

Published in 2007 by The Rosen Publishing Group, Inc.
29 East 21st Street, New York, NY 10010

Copyright © 2007 by The Rosen Publishing Group, Inc.

All rights reserved. No part of this book may be reproduced in any form without permission in writing from the publisher, except by a reviewer.

First Edition

Editor: Jennifer Way
Book Design: Greg Tucker
Photo Researcher: Sam Cha

Photo Credits: Cover, pp. 1, 6, 8, 10, 18, 21, 22, 27, 29, 30 © Otto Greule Jr./Getty Images; pp. 4, 16, 25 © Jonathan Ferrey/Getty Images; pp. 13, 14 © Tom Hauck/Allsport; pp. 10, 16 © Jamie Squire/Allsport; p. 23 © Elsa/Getty Images.

Library of Congress Cataloging-in-Publication Data

Smithwick, John.
  Meet Shaun Alexander : football's top running back / John Smithwick. — 1st ed.
      p. cm. — (All-star players)
  Includes index.
  ISBN-13: 978-1-4042-3635-6 (library binding)
  ISBN-10: 1-4042-3635-X (library binding)
  1. Alexander, Shaun—Juvenile literature. 2. Running backs (Football)—United States—Biography—Juvenile literature. I. Title.
  GV939.A48S65 2007
  796.332092—dc22
  [B]
                                                    2006019657

Manufactured in the United States of America

Contents

Shaun Alexander is a top NFL running back. His skills make him important to his team, the Seattle Seahawks.

Meet Shaun Alexander

Shaun Alexander is a running back for the Seattle Seahawks. A running back's job is to take the football and run. This is called rushing.

A good running back must be fast, but he must also be **agile**. Imagine running as fast as you can in one direction. Suddenly you have to change direction without slowing down. A running back must do this each time he has the football. This is how he avoids being **tackled** by the opposing team's **defense**.

A good running back also has to be strong. Some of the players who are trying to tackle him weigh more than 300 pounds (136 kg)! Shaun Alexander can do all these things and more. He is one of the best running backs ever to pick up a football.

Alexander's talent has brought him a
long way since his childhood in Kentucky.
Here he is rushing with the Seahawks.

Kentucky Childhood

Shaun Alexander was born on August 30, 1977. He grew up in a poor neighborhood in the town of Florence, Kentucky. He lived in a small apartment with his mother, Carol, and his brother, Durran. Carol raised both boys by herself. She was also a neighborhood leader. She helped people who were in trouble. She gave people food and money, even though she was poor herself. Carol Alexander taught the value of generosity to her children.

While they were growing up, both of the Alexander brothers learned that they were blessed with talents. Durran loved music and became an excellent drummer. Shaun was good at sports and played football for Boone County High School.

Alexander learned early how to keep cool under pressure. This is important when playing in the NFL.

Boone County High School takes football seriously. Ten thousand fans regularly pack its **stadium** to watch the games. This can mean a lot of **pressure** and attention on young players. Alexander rose to the occasion. He became one of the best high-school football players Kentucky has ever seen. He won the Kentucky State Player of the Year Award after his final season, in 1996. Alexander also set school records for rushing yards and touchdowns. He even set a nationwide touchdown record. It was no surprise when he was granted a football **scholarship** to the University of Alabama.

Alexander may not have won the Heisman, but he had the attention of NFL coaches.

The Crimson Tide

Shaun Alexander received his scholarship because he broke high-school football records. While playing for the Crimson Tide at the University of Alabama, he broke college football records.

In his freshman year, Alexander ran for 291 yards in a single game against Louisiana State University. He scored four touchdowns in the same game.

By his junior year in 1998, Alexander averaged over 100 yards per game. He was considered such a great player that many coaches and sports journalists urged him to skip his final year in college and start playing in the NFL. However, Alexander was **loyal** to his university, and he turned down millions of dollars to play his final year at Alabama.

All-Star Stats

Shaun Alexander continues to hold the Crimson Tide rushing record. In four seasons he rushed 3,565 yards.

It looked like Alexander would be having an excellent year. Alexander was on his way to winning the Heisman **Trophy**. The Heisman Trophy is named after the **legendary** coach John Heisman. He helped make football into the game we know today. Each year the trophy is given to the most outstanding college player. Sadly, Alexander hurt his ankle and did not play as well for the rest of the season after that. He did not win the Heisman, but he still helped the Crimson Tide claim their conference championship and a win in the Iron Bowl. After graduating as Alabama's all-time leading rusher with 3,565 yards, Alexander was ready for the NFL.

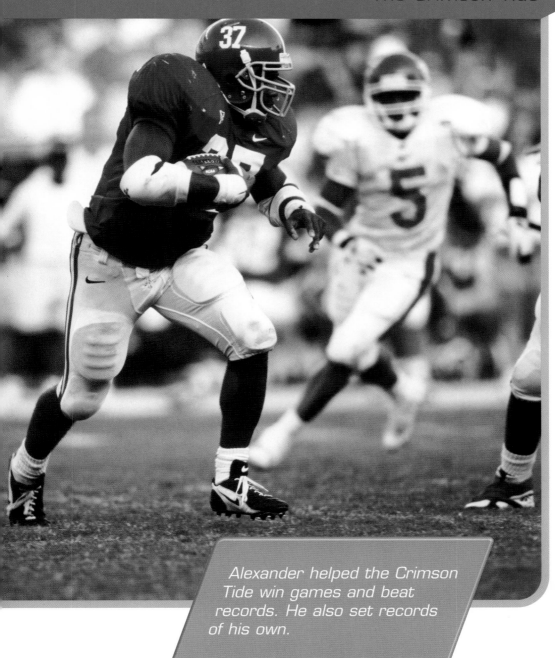

Alexander helped the Crimson Tide win games and beat records. He also set records of his own.

Alexander has come to enjoy living in Seattle and playing for the Seahawks.

Shaun Alexander entered the NFL draft in the spring of 2000. The draft is how the NFL teams choose the best college **athletes** to play for them. There are seven rounds in the draft. Each team gets to pick one player each round.

The sports **media** greatly values the first 10 players who are drafted. These 10 players are considered the best players in the draft. These players are expected to make immediate contributions to their new NFL teams.

Since Alexander's college football **career** was so remarkable, many journalists figured he would be among the first 10 players drafted. They were

All-Star Stats

It did not take Alexander very long to change his mind about his new town. He met a woman there named Valerie May, who soon became his wife.

He may not have been a top draft pick, but Alexander soon proved his worth to the Seahawks.

wrong. Alexander was the nineteenth player drafted. Three other running backs were picked before him. Alexander felt let down. To make it even worse, the Seattle Seahawks selected him, and they already had a good running back named Ricky Watters. It was clear that Alexander would be his backup.

The thought of moving all the way across the country to Seattle did not appeal to Alexander, either. Seattle was far away from everyone he knew. Alexander would soon find that he had made a smart move, though.

Alexander quickly became a popular Seahawk. Here he is waving to fans in 2005.

The Seattle Seahawks

In his first season with the Seahawks, in 2000, Shaun Alexander played every game. Since he was not the starting running back, his playing time in those games was limited.

In the 2001–2002 season, Ricky Watters was hurt during a game. Alexander had to step into the starting position. He rushed for 1,318 yards. In the NFL a running back's season is considered excellent if he rushes for 1,000 yards.

His performances over the next seasons were even better. He began to break NFL records. In 2002, Alexander set an NFL record by scoring five touchdowns in the first half of a game.

A year later Alexander rushed for 1,435 yards and scored 16 touchdowns. These accomplishments earned him his first appearance in the Pro Bowl. The Pro Bowl is a football game played by the best players from each team. Playing on a Pro Bowl team is considered an honor.

In 2004, Alexander topped his past successes yet again. He scored 20 touchdowns and rushed for 1,696 yards.

The 2005 season was Alexander's best yet. He led the league with 1,880 rushing yards and broke the single-season touchdown record with a total of 28 touchdowns. Alexander became the fourth running back in NFL history to score 20 or more touchdowns in back-to-back seasons. He was voted the NFL's Most Valuable Player. This means he did more for his team than any other player that year. He was also soon to lead the Seahawks to the Super Bowl.

Here is Alexander being tackled by Brandon Green of the St. Louis Rams.

The Seahawks had a great 2005–2006 season. Here Alexander avoids a tackle in a game against the San Francisco 49ers.

Super Bowl XL

Shaun Alexander entered the 2006 play-offs ready to lead the Seahawks to the Super Bowl. Seattle won the play-off game against the Washington Redskins, but Alexander was hit very hard during the game and suffered a **concussion**. The Seahawks were worried that Alexander might not be able to play for the rest of the play-offs.

Alexander and the Seahawks played the Pittsburgh Steelers in Super Bowl XL.

Alexander's **determination** proved to be greater than his **injury**. He quickly recovered and the Seahawks won all their play-off games. Now they had to face the Pittsburgh Steelers in Super Bowl XL, on February 5, 2006.

Unfortunately for Alexander and the Seahawks, the Steelers beat the Seahawks, 21 to 10. The game was much closer than the score makes it seem. Even though his team lost, Alexander was the game's leading rusher, with 95 yards. It was a good end to the best season of his career.

Super Bowl XL was a close game. Alexander was able to rush even while avoiding tackles, such as this one from Steeler Joey Porter.

The Shaun Alexander Foundation

Football is an important part of Shaun Alexander's life, but it is not the most important part of his life. Alexander remembers and values the generosity his mother taught him. Even while struggling to raise two children by herself, Carol Alexander became a **pillar** of her community. Her sons continue in her footsteps.

Shortly after the NFL draft, Alexander used some of the money the Seahawks paid him to start a charity. With the help of his brother, he created the Shaun Alexander Foundation. It provides **mentors** to youths who need help in school or in their lives. These mentors help teenagers stay in school and stay out of trouble.

Alexander likes to use his fame to help kids in poorer communities. Here he is speaking to reporters in 2006.

The Outlook for Alexander

In March 2006, Shaun Alexander signed a new contract with the Seahawks. He will play at least eight more years for them and receive $62 million. This contract makes Alexander the highest-paid running back in the history of the NFL. Since Alexander keeps improving each season, the Seahawks consider it a bargain.

Shaun Alexander now feels at home in Seattle. He loves his family even more than he loves playing football. He and his wife, Valerie, have two young daughters. The Alexanders hope to have six children total. They recently purchased a house big enough for all of them.

Alexander wants to be more than a great football player. He wants to be a great husband, a great father, and a pillar of his community.

Alexander will play with the Seahawks until 2014. In that time he hopes to bring the team to a Super Bowl win.

Height: 5'11" (1.8 m)
Weight: 225 pounds (102 kg)
Team: The Seattle Seahawks
Uniform Number: 37
Date of Birth: August 30, 1977
Draft Pick: 2000, first round
Years in the NFL: 7

2005–2006 Season Stats

Games Played	Rushes	Total Yards	Yards per Rush	Touchdowns
16	370	1,880	5.1	28

Career Stats as of 2005–2006 Season

Career Rushing Yards	Career Rushing Touchdowns
7,817	89

Glossary

agile (A-jul) Able to move easily and gracefully.

athletes (ATH-leets) People who take part in sports.

career (kuh-REER) A job.

concussion (kun-KUH-shun) Pain and other harm caused by a hard blow to the head.

defense (DEE-fents) When a team tries to stop the other team from scoring.

determination (dih-ter-mih-NAY-shun) Being firm in purpose.

injury (INJ-ree) Bodily harm or hurt done to a person.

legendary (LEH-jen-der-ee) Of or relating to a person who has been famous and honored for a very long time.

loyal (LOY-ul) Faithful to a person or an idea.

media (MEE-dee-uh) Journalists and people who appear on TV and radio shows.

mentors (MEN-torz) Trusted guides or teachers.

pillar (PIH-lur) A respected person.

pressure (PREH-shur) The weight of feeling worried about something.

scholarship (SKAH-ler-ship) Money given to someone to pay for school.

stadium (STAY-dee-um) A place where sports are played.

tackled (TA-kuld) To have stopped someone by knocking him down.

trophy (TROH-fee) A prize that is often made of metal and shaped like a cup.

Index

Web Sites

Due to the changing nature of Internet links, PowerKids Press has developed an online list of Web sites related to the subject of this book. This site is updated regularly. Please use this link to access the list:
www.powerkidslinks.com/asp/shaun/